Krampus: The History and Legacy of the Mythological Figure Who Scares Children during the Christmas Season

By Charles River Editors

A 19th century depiction of St. Nicholas and Krampus

About Charles River Editors

Charles River Editors is a boutique digital publishing company, specializing in bringing history back to life with educational and engaging books on a wide range of topics. Keep up to date with our new and free offerings with this 5 second sign up on our weekly mailing list, and visit Our Kindle Author Page to see other recently published Kindle titles.

We make these books for you and always want to know our readers' opinions, so we encourage you to leave reviews and look forward to publishing new and exciting titles each week.

Introduction

Krampus

Mattias Kabel's picture of someone dressed up as Krampus

"'Tis late night in Bavaria, and all through the village

The grownups are drunk, full of beer and such swillage;

While children a-tremble, hide deep in their beds,

Fearful the Krampus will rip off their heads." - Ann Hart, "Krampusnacht" (2016) "

Christmas is the most important holiday of the year. After the corresponding days that exalt the national pride of each country, such as Independence Day in the United States, Victory Day in Russia, or Bastille Day in France, it's December 25 that articulates the life, the work and the economy in much of the world, including many non-Christian countries. Since ancient times, the beginning of winter has been the occasion for most people to eat, drink, dance, and get together to beat the drum and take a break.

One of the aspects of Christmas that is most famous is Santa Claus, a mythological figure with many monikers, such as Kris Kringle, Father Christmas, and Papai Noel, among others. Pop culture enthusiasts know to trace Santa's roots to Saint Nicholas, and it's widely accepted that Coke manufactured the contemporary image of Santa embraced by the world today. On both counts, they are only partially correct, because in reality, Santa is a colorful amalgamation of different figures who appear in various countries' folk stories across a wide range of centuries.

Though Santa had many influences, his most famous is St. Nicholas, a fiercely religious philanthropist who dedicated his life to helping the disadvantaged. He was not just a beloved bishop, but a fierce defender of the faith who remained undaunted in the face of persecution. To brand him a pious and God-fearing individual would be a massive understatement – indeed, he was, to those around him, the definition of a walking divinity, and an unrivaled miracle-worker sent straight from Heaven.

After Nicholas of Myra's death, December 6 became his feast day, and over the centuries, children anticipated his appearance with gifts. However, other children, particularly those of the mischievous sort, trembled under their covers on December 6, because they could no tlook forward to tinkling sleigh bells or belly-shaking laughs. Instead, they feared the disconcerting sounds of heavy breathing, guttural growls, and rattling chains, all of which came from the terrifying Krampus.

Despite the best efforts of the Catholic Church and other conservative groups, Krampus is in the midst of a major Renaissance, penetrating not only modern literature, but even becoming a fixture of pop culture. This is evidenced by the creature's recent starring roles in the films *Krampus*, *Night of the Krampus*, and *Mother Krampus*, and its cameos in such TV shows and animations as Grimm, Supernatural, American Dad, and Venture Brothers.

Krampus: The History and Legacy of the Mythological Figure Who Punishes Children during the Christmas Season examines the pagan and Christian influences of the Yuletide villain, and dives into the riveting and frightening history behind the creature. Along with pictures depicting important people, places, and events, you will learn about Krampus like never before.

Krampus: The History and Legacy of the Mythological Figure Who Punishes Children during the Christmas Season

About Charles River Editors

Introduction

    A Pagan Pedigree

    Krampusnacht and Christian Influences

    Krampus Leaves the Alps

    Krampus in the Modern Age

    Online Resources

    Further Reading

Free Books by Charles River Editors

Discounted Books by Charles River Editors

A Pagan Pedigree

Every Advent, the idyllic church town of Salzburg is transformed into a truly bewitching winter wonderland. The streets, steeples, and rooftops are dusted with a rich, yet delicate layer of snow. Daylight is fleeting and the frost in the air nips at one's skin, but the golden garlands of fairy lights floating above the streets and the shimmering ornaments adorning towering Christmas trees provide both ample illumination and a whisper of whimsy. Around every corner, it seems, temptation awaits. Christmas markets with colorful booths large and small are a magnet for children, and the scenes awaken the inner child of even the most hardened adults. On top of the Christmas-themed floral arrangements, wreaths, tree ornaments, and endless arrays of handmade toys and trinkets, one is greeted by the fanciful sight of fruit loafs, sugary pastries, frosted biscuits, chocolates, and toffee apples, as well as hot chocolate and eggnog dispensers, and extensive selections of mulled wine, punch, and holiday-flavored liqueurs.

This picturesque equation is completed as people make their way back to their cabins, experiencing the rhythmic crunching of the snow under their boots and the seductive scent of freshly baked goods still wafting out of darkened bakeries. But, as Plato once said, things are not always what they seem. It can be quiet, almost too quiet, and the stringed lights above begin to flicker. Logic dictates that the city's power appears to be close to overheating. More distressing yet, everyone else seems to have cleared out of the streets, yet it is difficult to shake the feeling that those who have remained are not alone. And that's when they hear the grating toll of rusty cow bells and the disquieting rattling of heavy chains, followed by a guttural snarl and the ominous tread of cloven hooves.

This wintertime fiend is none other than the infamous Krampus, otherwise known by the contemporary nicknames, "The Christmas Devil" and the "Demon Anti-Santa." Chances are that those outside of the Alpine region in Europe have only heard of this holiday antihero in passing, if at all. Given Krampus' ghastly activities, it is not difficult to imagine why the controversial character has been scrubbed out of the traditionally Christian Christmas traditions and excluded from the saccharinely wholesome backstory of Santa Claus pushed by the commercial executives of today.

While Krampus has made something of a comeback in recent years and is now considered a cult figure in certain circles around the globe, the significance of this often misunderstood wintertime creature continues to be severely understated. In reality, Krampus is far more than a seasonal bogeyman manufactured by parents to keep their kids in line – he is an irreplaceable component of the Yuletide pantheon with a riveting history, and Krampus has become a symbol so professedly dark that the creature was outlawed by Christian groups and political parties alike.

Many today assume that Krampus or the idea of Krampus was born in Austria, but while Krampus was certainly popularized by Austria and other Alpine regions, it is difficult to pinpoint Krampus' exact origins. Historians believe that Krampus is an eclectic fusion of characters –

most often antagonists – plucked from millennia-old pagan folklore from various parts of the continent. That said, it is important to remember that the source material linking Krampus to the following folkloric personalities are far and few between.

First and foremost, most scholars begin by breaking down the etymology of the Christmas demon's name. The moniker "Krampus" is most likely a derivative of *"kralle,"* the Middle Germanic term for "claw," or perhaps the Bavarian word *"krampn,"* which alludes to something withered, wilted, and devoid of life. It is therefore only natural for historians to connect the dots between Krampus and the concept of death.

The most widely accepted theory views Krampus as the bastardization of the Norse goddess Hel, sometimes referred to as "Hela." Hel was the youngest offspring of the shape-shifting trickster god Loki, and a fierce, but beautiful giantess named Angrboda, thereby making Hel the sister of the vicious sentient sea serpent Jormungand and the red-eyed wolf beast Fenrir. Together, they were one of the most formidable and aptly forbidding families in all the Nine Worlds of Yggdrasil.

The duality of Krampus' biology – part demon, part goat – was possibly inspired by the frightening polarity in the goddess' appearance. Hel was petrifying to look at, described as "a horrible hag, half alive and half dead, with a gloomy and grim expression." In some accounts, her upper half is that of a ravishing young maiden with soft golden locks that stopped at her waist. The beautiful torso, however, was attached to a pair of rotting legs with worms and maggots wriggling out of her porous, greenish-black flesh. In other accounts, Hel was split down the middle.

A 20ᵗʰ century depiction of Hel

As dictated by legend, it was Loki who was responsible for his daughter's disfigurement. When Hel was just a young girl, she became the subject of a horrid, but crucial ritual. Loki bound her limbs to two trees close to the bank, and forcibly submerged half of her body – in some versions, waist-down, and in others, flat on her side – in the frigid lake. Hel was left in this sorry state for days on end.

Her father eventually returned to unwind the ropes, but by then, the poisons of frostbite had already consumed half of her unconscious body. Loki acted fast, tipping her head back and pouring a special potion that would accelerate her faint heartbeat and salvage the dry half of her body. The ritual may have marred her for eternity, but her dance with death gifted her with the "second sight," one that allowed her to penetrate the realm of the dead and see "the shadows of the world beyond ours." Herein lies the second connection between Krampus and Hel, the latter an all-knowing and all-seeing goddess drawn to all that is dark and wicked.

With her new powers, she was appointed "overseer of the non-living" and the queen of Helheim (according to other accounts, Nilfheim), the Norse realm of the dead. She was expected to control and prevent the escape of the wretched souls that dwelt in this realm, primarily those taken by "old age, disease, and corruption." Any soul that managed to claw its way out of Helheim was promptly dragged back to the underworld and gravely disciplined.

Hel also emerged from Helheim on her winged, three-legged pet stallion, known only as the "Hel horse," during times of war and outbreaks of the plague and other diseases. She prowled through the smoke-filled streets, her rake (or a magical staff) clutched in her fist, stalking, capturing, and whisking survivors off to the underworld. Here, we see the third and fourth links between Krampus and Hel. Hel was the gatekeeper of Helheim with an appetite for wicked and hapless souls, whereas Krampus is seen as the guardian of the North Pole with a taste for misbehaving children. Furthermore, the silhouette of Hel seated upon the Hel horse may have also served as the muse behind Krampus' half-goat, half-demon appearance.

One of the most oft-repeated tales tied to Hel shows more parallels to the subtext in Krampus' constitution. When Balder, the son of the chief god, Odin, and the goddess of wisdom, Frigg, was murdered by Loki via a spear to the heart, his soul was imprisoned in the Helheim hall called "Eljudnir." On the back of Odin's eight-legged horse, Sleipnir, Balder's brother Hermod arranged a meeting with Hel to negotiate the return of his brother. Hel was initially hesitant, but the pair eventually brokered an ultimatum.

Hel would only release Balder from her lair if each and every living and non-living creature in all the Nine Worlds properly demonstrated their grief for the fallen god. Eventually, Hermod succeeded in convincing all deities, mortals, and even animals to play along, except for one. An ugly and cruel giantess by the name of Thokk, said to be one of Loki's countless disguises, refused to humor the gods who had come to plead Balder's case, adamantly shedding only "waterless tears." And so, Hel held onto Balder, where he remained until the final destruction of the world, an event known as Ragnarok. Hel and Krampus were ferocious, but fair; they kept to their word, and they punished those that disobeyed them.

Conversely, some believe that Krampus was not an alternate version of Hel but the spawn of Hel, making him the grandson of Loki. That being said, the details of Krampus' conception and the identity of his father remain a mystery. Krampus was confined to the icy depths of Nilfheim. Here, he remained for 364 days of the year, but on the coldest day of winter, he escaped from his dreadful lair and entered the realm of the mortals, hunting for delinquent youths and unruly children.

Krampus is also said to be the descendant of the Alpine pagan goddess Frau Perchta, the ancient Yuletide witch and the muse behind the 2017 thriller and box office flop *Mother Krampus*. A native of the Upper German and Austrian portions of the Alpine region, Perchta was a shape-shifter that came in two forms, either as an attractive young woman with flowing curls as white as lace, or an elderly, unkempt crone with sunken features, bloodshot eyes, matted clumps of frizzy white hair, and gruesome scars etched across her wrinkled skin. Whatever the form, she was recognizable by her hideous, oversized foot.

Like Krampus, Perchta – described as the embodiment of Epiphany – was equipped with the powers of judge, jury, and executioner. The swan-footed goddess recompensed the do-gooders and doled out vengeful punishments to those who lied, cheated, hoarded, idled, and killed. She was most vindictive towards those who failed to properly venerate her on her feast day, known as *Perchttag* ("Perchta Day") or "Epiphany."

As maintained by Epiphany customs, all mortals were expected to refrain from any form of work. Offerings of mead and the finest crops of the latest harvest aside, families and neighbors were obligated to spend quality time together. Families sat in a circle around their hearths and tucked into filling meals of roasted fish and gruel. Afterwards, they headed out to the village square, where they toasted glasses of mead and exchanged stories.

To label the punishment she meted out to workaholics and introverts excessive and grossly inordinate would be an understatement. Those who failed to halt their spinning wheels and socialize with family and friends were visited by Perchta that very same evening. She crept in through open windows and hobbled over to her slumbering victims. Sometimes, they were awoken by the thumps of her swan foot, or the screech of her knife dragging across the floor, but by then, it was too late. She clamped her shriveled hand onto the mouths of her victims to stifle their screams, and in one swift motion, sliced open their stomachs. She then yanked out their intestines like a never-ending handkerchief and stuffed their stomachs with straw, pebbles, rotten apple cores, and other pieces of garbage.

An early 20th century depiction of Perchta from the Kingdom of Bohemia

Perchta was only tolerant of indolence on her feast day. The rest of the year, mortals, young and old, were to be diligent in their duties at school or work. Similar to Krampus, Perchta did not discriminate when it came to discipline, and her punishments were no lighter on children. The pair were a breed the Germans called *Kinderschrek,* meaning "one that frightens children." Perchta especially detested children who lied and cheated. Lie again, parents warned their dishonest children, and Perchta would come in the middle of the night to cut up their tongues with a shard of glass, while repeat offenders had their entire tongues sawed off. Unlike Krampus, however, who is only known to make an example of trouble-making children, Perchta placed a silver coin by the pillows of the hard-working and the well-behaved.

Historians who support this theory believe that Krampus was birthed from the latter species of Perchta's phantom entourage, the *Schönperchten,* which roughly translates to "beautiful souls," and the *Schiachperchten*, or in English, "ugly souls." Whereas the *Schönperchten* were composed of enchanting nymphs, fetching fairies, and other delightful creatures, the *Schiachperchten*, to which Krampus belonged, were unbaptized souls and hairy, horned beasts with jagged rows of sharp, blade-like teeth, coupled with human-like torsos and the legs of either a goat or a horse. Perchta and her retinue embarked on excursions in the realm of the mortals twice a year, once during the 12 days before Christmas, and again in the 12 days leading up to her feast day. Only by presenting the appropriate offerings would one be paid a visit from the ghostly retinue, who flitted from door to door to evict evil spirits, poltergeists, and demons and rid homes of negative energy.

The parallels between them have led a few to believe that Perchta and Krampus may be one and the same, but while they are cut from the same cloth, they are most likely separate entities with feast days almost a month apart from one another. While Perchta's falls on the 6th of January, Krampus' is the 5th of December. Some chroniclers have also referred to Perchta as the female romantic companion of Krampus.

Like Santa Claus, Krampus may have also been a byproduct of the pagan *Wilde Jagd*, or "Wild Hunt" tradition. In essence, Wild Hunts were similar to the wintertime expeditions Perchta and her cortege undertook to perform their spiritual exorcisms. This crew of "wild hunters," which consisted of fairies, sprites, elves, and otherworldly spirits, was headed by the principal Norse god Odin.

The mortals dreaded the coming of the Wild Hunt, as they were believed to augur an incoming war, an outbreak of an infectious disease, or some other form of bloodshed. Moreover, they made certain to vacate the streets and lock themselves in their homes by dusk, for those who happened upon the deadly train of wild souls were abducted and swept off to the underworld. The living also made certain to hang squares of black cloth over their bedroom windows, for maleficent spirits who broke away from the pack were known to slink in and suck out the souls of mortals, forcing them to forever partake in the procession. Here, one finds another association between Krampus and the phantoms of the Wild Hunt, as the former is also said to kidnap ill-behaved children and haul them off to his lair.

In order to keep these odious specters at arm's length, ancient European mortals developed a winter solstice tradition now referred to as "mummery." Villagers donned elaborate costumes and masks that resembled various animals and mythological creatures and spilled into the streets. The costumed villagers paraded around the village, dancing – mostly sans choreography – and chanting monotonously. The idea was to camouflage themselves; by blending in, the shadowy hunters mistook them for other members of the spectral retinue and left them to their own devices. In doing so, the performers were also able to deceive and cast out the wicked spirits lurking in their homes. The most common characters featured in these pagan mummeries were

Old Man Winter and the Horned Goat Man, who historians believe later evolved into Santa and Krampus, respectively.

Villagers who subscribed to Perchta also partook in a similar procession. Half of the Perchten – the name for these masked folk performers – disguised themselves as *Schiachperchten*, which shared many physical features with what they would soon call the *"Krampusse."*

The Perchten wore full-body suits fashioned out of sheep pelts or goatskins, which were then dyed in dark colors and covered with bits of hair to give the appearance of filthy, mangy fur. They accessorized with massive bells, which dangled from their belts, and carried bundles of tree branches and twigs, or switches made from cow tails or horsehair. The hefty hand-painted wooden masks worn by the Perchten usually featured the heads of wolves, eagles, bears, and other beasts, but those donned by "devils," supposedly Krampus, were decorated with horns, tusks, fangs, and protruding tongues. A few mask makers opted to leave the ears out of their portrayals of the *Schiachperchten* devils. Some believed these beasts were born this way, and attribute their malignancy to their lack of ears, as they are unable to hear the screams of their victims. The aforementioned theatrical processions, as well as the practice of mask-making also served as precursors to Krampus traditions still upheld to this day.

Mattias Kabel's picture of a Perchta mask

Krampus storytellers may have also incorporated elements from the ancient pagan belief of household spirits. These house-bound spirits guarded one's home, and were either attached to a single member of, or the entire family, typically upon, or shortly after the day of the mortals' arrival. As opposed to other deities, mortals did not create separate temples to honor these creatures; rather, a small and well-attended shrine devoted to them was set up inside the mortals' homes, usually by the hearth.

Veneration methods varied from household to household. The more superstitious families habitually whipped up an extra meal for the spirit at the dining table throughout the year. Most families, however, only prepared offerings for these spirits on special celebrations, which included either a helping of each dish served at a feast, or gifts of milk, wine, honey, incense, fruits, sweet cakes, and on occasion, a blood sacrifice. These treats were either placed on platters atop an unlit hearth, or a nearby mantle in an empty room, which allowed for privacy. Herein lies another link to Krampus, who must also be honored with a gift of food and drink.

These peace offerings placated the household spirits. Once again, unlike Krampus, the spirits occasionally demonstrated their gratitude by helping out with chores, such as dusting, sweeping, repairing broken furniture and tools, and tending to the animals on the farm. Some even hid coins and valuables around the house that had been pilfered from neighbors. Those who failed to present said offerings had no choice but to face the wrath of these house-dwelling spirits. These unforgiving phantoms went out of their way to harass the family members, shattering dishes in the middle of the night and yanking off the blankets draped over sleeping children, among other pranks.

Krampus is believed to be an offshoot of a type of household spirit called the "kobold." The kobold's appearance differed from region to region. In some localities, they were depicted as pint-sized, spooky elves with oversized pointed ears, beady eyes, and bulbous, hooked noses, often paired with a pipe in hand. In other regions, they were portrayed as upright reptilian creatures with large, webbed feet, dressed in rags found lying around the house, and armed with miniature spears, whips, and wooden cages attached to sticks, much like a bindle. In certain Alpine regions, kobolds were also said to come in the form of various animals and beasts, such as the drac, which was reminiscent of a sphinx – a creature with the head of an elderly, bearded man and the body of a lion. The Krampus' appearance, some historians believe, was based on this particular version of the kobold.

Kobolds set up camp in the nooks and niches of homes, most often in attics and underground cellars. Historians believe that kobolds, not unlike hobgoblins, drew some inspiration from the Anglo-Saxon *cofgodas*, AKA "cove gods," who were known to dwell in cupboards and other corners of the house. Whereas the kobolds left behind confetti of sawdust and wood chips on the floor, Krampus left behind pools of crimson, trails of dirt, and claw marks leading to either the hearth or the bedroom window.

The kobolds, some say, were the most difficult to please, and more alarmingly, the most sadistic of all the household spirits. Irritating, but ultimately harmless pranks were not enough for the kobolds to rest on their laurels. They captured disobedient family members and hacked off their limbs and returned to detach more limbs for every repeat offense. Some, legend has it, were flung into roaring bonfires; others asphyxiated in the homes set ablaze by the murderous kobolds. The similarities regarding the relentless mean streak and the punishment methods of the Krampus and kobolds must also be noted.

The fauns, satyrs, and centaurs from ancient mythology are also visibly present in Krampus' composition. Fauns, a product of Roman lore, stemmed from chimeras – a name given to a fire-breathing beast with the head of a lion, the body of a goat, and the tail of a serpent – but were mostly equipped with a man's torso and a goat's body. Like Krampus, fauns were adorned with horns and accoutered with furry, bent legs, hooves, and a restless tail. Unlike Krampus, however, the human halves of fauns were incredibly handsome, with full heads of shiny curls, twinkling eyes, taut skin, and youthful smirks. According to the Romans, fauns were strapping, energetic, musical, and outdoorsy creatures with an insatiable lust for beautiful female mortals.

Their chimeric cousins, the *Satyroi,* or satyrs, shared their love for desirable maidens. In comparison with the fauns, however, satyrs were fiercer, rustic countryside creatures who fraternized with the nymphs and often accompanied Hermes, Hephaistos, Dionysos, Gaia, and other gods and goddesses. The satyr's physical appearance was more analogous to that of Krampus as opposed to the fauns, for their human halves were embellished with asinine (donkey) ears, goat horns, large, crooked noses, and a hairline that began only halfway across the skull. Then, there was the most glaring part of their anatomy – the massive appendages between their legs, which were fully erect at all times. Krampus may have not been particularly, if at all, fond of nature or music, but the creature's physical features, as well as its bizarre side of lechery, is believed to have been derived from the lustful nature of the fauns and satyrs.

Some Wiccans have also laid claim to the origins of Krampus, who is supposedly the progeny of the Horned God of the Witches. As maintained by these Wiccans, the Horned God – which predated even the notion of Satan – served as the source of inspiration behind the duality of Krampus' appearance, as well as its horns and hooves. According to them, Christians only added the ram or stag-like horns, hooves, wings, and the bestial legs to the description of Satan sometime in the Middle Ages. Indeed, Krampus is most similar in appearance to the Horned God/Satan, given the long, narrow, and hooked horns, asinine ears, and iconic goat hooves. As Maurice Bruce put it, "There seems to be little doubt as to his true identity for, in no other form is the full regalia of the Horned God of the Witches so well preserved. The birch – apart from its phallic significance – may have a connection with the initiation rites of certain witch-covens; rites which entailed binding and scourging as a form of mock-death. The chains could have been introduced in a Christian attempt to 'bind the Devil' but again they could be a remnant of pagan initiation rites."

On top of the striking physical resemblances between them, the Horned God, crowned as the "lord of life, death, and the underworld," was born at winter solstice. The Horned God had a binary role; not only was a necessary half in the process of the fertility cycle of birth, death, and rebirth, but the Wiccans counted on him to provide wild game and other means of sustenance. The Horned God was the male counterpart to the Goddess and a requisite constituent of the "divine duality," ensuring the delicate balance of life on Earth, much like Krampus is often described as the yin to Santa's yang.

A picture of a Krampus in Croatia

Krampusnacht and Christian Influences

Due to the Roman conquests, particularly in the 4th century CE, more and more Germanic tribes were converted to Christianity. A few sparsely populated villages along the Alps, however, managed to circumvent the mainstream. They held onto their traditional pagan beliefs and practiced their heathen customs away from prying eyes, allowing for the gradual evolution of Krampus and the traditions associated with the wintertime bogeyman.

The original Krampus would have been a formless beast with constantly changing features, for this imaginary Yuletide villain was painted only by the variable descriptions provided by parents and storytellers, as passed down by oral tradition. As time progressed, the Alpine villages that remained dedicated to Krampus began to further flesh out his physical appearance and backstory.

Still, every region stayed faithful to their own renditions of the Krampus. Author Robert Lamb explained, "[Krampus'] exact appearance varies depending on time, place, and available costuming materials. In fact, the more you explore the nature of Krampus, the more you come to see him as a byproduct of accumulated beliefs, traditions, and primal fears."

By the end of the medieval period, a cohesive image of Krampus had been formed, one that is still used as a reference by artists and animators in the 21st century. The monstrous Krampus is a towering, powerfully built figure, thickly coated from head to toe in black or brown fur. The lower half of its body was that of a two-legged goat, one fitted with a cloven hoof, and the other with sharp, yellow claws attached to a large, human-like foot, as well as a long and thick tail ending in a paintbrush-like clump of fur. The upper half of its sculpted body, though covered with fur, was human, as are the arms and hands, but the nails on its opposable fingers are razor-sharp and claw-like.

As hideous as that all was, it was Krampus' head that young ones considered the stuff of nightmares. Menacing antlers (or horns) aside, the beast has a narrow face and a goat-like, pointed chin, paired with round, lidless, and therefore unblinking yellow eyes, and a wide, snarling mouth stretched from one ear to the other, packed with disconcertingly sharp fangs stained from the flesh and blood of its all-meat diet. More unnerving yet, Krampus' teeth failed to cage its slimy, seemingly unending tongue, and as such, it leaves foul-smelling, gooey trails of saliva in its path. The creature can determine a child's behavior and the purity of their inner thoughts with just a quick swipe of its tongue. Despite of Krampus' unusually large tongue, the creature, according to various Alpine legends, is surprisingly well-spoken.

Krampus, who apparently smells of burnt coal, sulfur, and the usual aromas associated with hellfire, is also seen lugging around a lengthy chain link, often attached to a miserable queue of child captives. In other depictions, it carries around this chain – an accessory enforced by Christians, so as to symbolize "the binding of the Devil" – as a weapon. Cow bells are also clipped onto the creature's belt, presumably to signal its arrival. Most of the time, however, Krampus is armed with twig switches, as well as a portable washtub, basket, or empty sack strapped to its back.

Interestingly, the context clues in the descriptions provided of Krampus over the years led some zoologists to wonder whether Krampus had been an actual animal, perhaps a particularly evasive, unrecognizable species that few have seen in the wild. Given Krampus' oft-mentioned fangs and its apparent tendency to snack on children, one can gather that this potential creature was carnivorous in diet. Krampus' long, meandering tongue – which legend says furls around the body of children, allowing for effortless snatching – hints at either a serpentine creature, or possibly an antediluvian hybrid of an anteater, which is equipped with a tongue roughly two feet in length, and some other carnivorous mammal. The animal would have certainly been a hulking, brawny mammal, considering its appetite for children, but why the animal would require such a lengthy tongue when it could have easily killed its prey via mauling or neck-breaking is a mystery.

On the other hand, Robert Lamb offers another theory: "But perhaps Krampus is something else entirely: a hoofed carnivore descended from the extinct order *Mesonychid,* predatory land ungulates – or a relative of the long-extinct *Artiodactyla Andrewsarchus*, which some paleontologists interpret as a cloven-hoofed carnivore. Perhaps the balance is a bipedal omnivore that feasts on abundant greens in the summer and cruelly-won meat in the winter – a notion that fits well into Krampus' legacy as a monster born of winter survivalism [sic] and post-harvest anxiety."

When digging deeper into the stories surrounding Krampus, however, it seems quite clear that the Krampus manufactured by millennia of accumulated lore is no animal, at least not a real one.

An early 20th century depiction of Krampus and children

    While the sexless beast is often portrayed as a revolting hell-hound laced with diabolic themes, it is fair-minded and scrupulous in its judgment and the execution of its activities. Courteous children who honored their parents need not fear Krampus, while irreverent and errant children, on the other hand, had good reason to tremble in their boots. Though Krampus is generally believed to be even-handed by nature, certain accounts claim that the creature had a propensity to bait children into misbehaving during slow seasons. When Krampus failed to do so, it was forced to sustain itself on the fear of impressionable children.

Wayward children are disciplined according to the severity of their disobedience. On the lowest tier is the penalty most frequently associated with Krampus – spankings and whippings via its weapon of choice: a bundle of birch rods, also referred to as "*ruten*." Incidentally, the significance of these birch rods dates back to pre-Christian pagan times, particularly in Wiccan circles. The deliberately phallic undercurrent of Krampus' favorite weapon was supposedly a meaningful element that had been woven into the rituals – more specifically, death reenactments – practiced by these witch covens. These evidently phallic birch rods may have also been an homage to the satyrs' eternally erect members.

On the second tier is a mode of punishment reserved for disobedient children who are trapped in the cycle of relapse. Similar to another Germanic bogeyman, known only as the "Man With the Sack," Krampus twines its tongue around the misbehaving child, scoops them out of their bed, and into the basket. The abducted child is then taken to Krampus' squalid and malodorous lair, supposedly situated in an obscure and inaccessible Alpine cave, where they remained captive for at least a year; the number of repeat offenses may also bear some impact on the child's sentence. According to other accounts, Krampus' lair is located somewhere amidst the fiery bowels of the underworld. This unsettling act of retribution, historians believe, was kindled by the real-life horror stories of Moorish invaders capturing European civilians and pawning them off as slaves.

The final tier of punishment – a gruesome and excruciatingly painful death – is devoted to children who are so abominable and irredeemable that even their parents have washed their hands of them. These children are not simply devoured, which would be a far too quick and painless death for Krampus' liking. Instead, they are made to endure a series of grisly tortures. These rotten apples are maimed beyond recognition. Their limbs are snapped off one at a time, as are their ears and eyeballs, which Krampus then consumes like hors d'oeuvres.

Krampus relishes these pleas for mercy and takes great pleasure in tormenting its deserving victims. It spends the months leading up to winter mulling over and designing new torture tactics, each more ghoulishly creative than the last. It enjoys twisting and tweaking the ears of young children, and ripping off pigtails, leaving behind bloody bald spots. Like Frau Perchta, Krampus is also fond of slashing open the bellies of squirming children and wolfing down their innards, all the while keeping its victim alive. As soon as Krampus grows weary of the child's cries for clemency and forgiveness, the creature tears off the child's tongue and swallows it.

When the child can be tortured no more, Krampus disposes of them. Normally, the beast ultimately feasts on the child and picks the bones clean, but Krampus' belly, unlike Santa's sack of gifts, is not bottomless. In such cases, the creature leads the shackled children to a remote cliff in the Alps and shoves them over the edge. Krampus is also known to drown children in local bodies of water, and at times, in symbolic pools of ink. The corpses and spirits of these children are then retrieved (via pitchfork) and collected and placed aboard a spectral train destined for the "Lake of Fire."

The feast day of Krampus falls on the 5th of December every year. To children, it is a bittersweet festivity now known as "*Krampusnacht,*" or in English, "Krampus Night." That said, sightings of this Yuletide beast begin as early as the last days of November. Krampus continues to roam the streets until the second week of December, when it then returns to the glacial Alps and ducks back into its cave, where it remains for the rest of the year.

Like *Perchttag, Krampusnacht* was originally commemorated by familial gatherings and sacred offerings. On Krampus Night, even those who lived in distant lands returned home, where they feasted and ignited the Yule log with their families. Following a glorious dinner consisting of succulent meats and rich, honeyed pastries, children prepared baskets overflowing with either salted meat or crops, which were then laid by the hearth, or next to the line of boots by the front door and left overnight. Next to this basket was a separate chalice of wine, usually brewed in the backyard. In later years, the wine offering was replaced by a tumbler of schnapps, a type of distilled fruit brandy, said to be the creature's favorite beverage.

Krampus may seem like an invincible and worryingly immortal being, but the creature does have two weaknesses. First, fruit offerings presented by a child – including, but not limited to oranges or apples – were usually enough to assuage its appetite. The gifts may even pique its generosity - a contented Krampus is known to share its treats with the child, if spotted, and may even engage the young one in civil and pleasant conversation. Once Krampus had guzzled down the treats, the creature would slink back out of the house, leaving the child unharmed.

For the most part, however, Krampus slipped in and out of the house at night without ever being detected. Children awoke the next morning to find the basket gone and the chalice drained dry. More often than not, the miserly Krampus left nothing in return for the offerings, but the fact that the children had been left sound and intact was gift enough. Whatever the case, such offerings, in Krampus' eyes, were compulsory, and it is known to have penalized well-behaved children who failed to fulfill their deferential duties.

Even when Krampus was feeling charitable, the creature's gift – if one can even call it that – was dismal. Occasionally, the beast left a single birch rod in the boot or stocking of the well-behaved child to serve as a reminder to maintain their good deportment throughout the upcoming year.

Fortunately, Krampus' gifts, though still somewhat somber, began to perk up towards the latter half of the 20th century. A 1958 article entitled "The Krampus in Styria," authored by Maurice Bruce, references the bundles of birch rods, hand-painted in gold, that were gifted to children in Styria (a state in southern Austria). Parents of the children mounted the emblematic birch bundle onto the wall of their living rooms, and at times, in the children's bedrooms, as a year-round reminder of Krampus' coming arrival. Bruce noted that "in those houses where the behavior of the children merits the application of corporal correction." These gilded birch rods, some say, are the forerunners of the Elf on the Shelf.

Although *Krampusnacht* was primarily centered on children, the adults orchestrated and participated in the revelry issued into the wee hours of the evening. In a move more akin to Halloween than Christmas, grownups dressed in crude costumes fabricated out of animal pelts, complete with horns, masks, chains, bells, and floppy tongue, and took to the streets on Krampus Night. They charged up and down the near-deserted roads en masse, rattling their chains and howling like manic demons as they chased children and rebellious teenagers still loitering after hours into their homes. Even obedient children, who were already snugly tucked into bed, shivered under their covers at the sound of the thunderous roars outside of their bedroom windows. This late-night and often booze-fueled marathon on *Krampusnacht* is now known as "*Krampuslauf*," or the "Krampus Run."

The *Krampuslauf* is now believed to be inspired by two ancient and rather peculiar celebrations: the pagan Roman festival "Saturnalia" and the "Feast of Fools," which was observed throughout Europe in medieval times. To begin with, Saturnalia, the most popular festival in pagan Rome, was consecrated to Saturn, the god of generation, wealth, agriculture, liberation, and time. The lively celebrations commenced on the 17th of December and lasted until the 24th, wrapping up with the *Dies Natalis Solis Invicti,* or the "Anniversary of Sol Invictus."

On the day of the anniversary, every household in the city, including the houses of government, engaged in a kind of symbolic role play. For 24 hours, slaves enjoyed pure, uninhibited freedom, while their masters were transformed into servants and made to cater to the whimsies of their temporary masters. A slave was even selected to reign for a day, and this mock monarch was known as the "*Saturnalicius princeps,*" the "Lord of Misrule," supposedly a name that would later become associated with Krampus. This swapping of roles, which represented the upending of the societal hierarchy and a detachment from established norms, was done in honor of Saturn, "the black sun," possibly a reference to natural cycles and changing seasons.

Centuries later, European clergymen launched the "Feast of Fools," a festival that strongly echoed the Saturnalia, to celebrate the final days of the year. In certain churches, mainly in France, clergymen organized ceremonies – attended by all in the village – to elect their own version of the "Lord of Misrule," whom they called the "King" or "Bishop of Fools." The attendees were then required by tradition to adhere to the oftentimes ludicrous commands of the false king. Curiously, this event was more secular than it was religious, as evidenced by the liberality and frankly, absurdity, of the king's demands.

An unnamed theologian described one such Feast: "Priests and clerks may be seen wearing masks and monstrous visages at the hours of office. They dance in the choir dressed as women, panders, or minstrels. They sing wanton songs. They eat black puddings...while the celebrant is saying Mass. They play [sic] at dice...They run and leap through the church, without a blush at their own shame..."

It is no coincidence that *Krampusnacht* falls on the eve of Saint Nicholas of Myra's feast day. This is a practice that many historians believe was enforced by the Catholic Church, which began in the early years of the Middle Ages and was revived in the 17th century. Pagan Perchten professions eventually evolved into Christian *Nikolosspiele*, or "Nicholas Plays," starring both Saint Nicholas and Krampus, initially depicted as the "Devil" or the "Horned Goat Man."

A 20th century procession featuring St. Nicholas and Krampus

6. December

An Austrian depiction of St. Nicholas and Krampus

A depiction of St. Nicholas and Krampus visiting a child

The first Nicholas Plays were what mummery experts now call the "freilauf," or "free runs," a parade style characterized by unorganized and unstructured dancing and movement. Molly Carter, author of "Perchten and Krampusse: Living Mask Traditions in Austria and Bavaria," shines a brighter light unto the topic in the following passage: "Mummers [in Nicholas Plays] move freely around the space, mingling with the crowd, making use of environmental features to improvise, such as leaping off low walls and sneaking up behind people. They make the most of the opportunity to return to favorite victims, known and unknown, noted and perhaps engaged with fleetingly during the parade, initiating or developing the performance-encounter with them.

Acting as individuals and free from the time and space constraints of more structured performance settings (such as parades and plays), mummers are thus able to further personalize and elaborate upon their performance ideas."

This brings up the widely misinterpreted relationship between Saint Nicholas and Krampus, reputedly the latter's second weakness. Time and time again, Krampus is misconstrued as the anti-Santa, the arch nemesis of the beloved and benevolent Saint Nicholas. In actuality, Krampus is Santa's right-hand man, the bad cop to Kris Kringle's good cop.

Traditionally, parents collaborated with friends and neighbors, arranging house visits on the 5th of every December from Saint Nicholas and Krampus. This custom, now known as the "*Einkehrbrauch*," was popularized in the early 1700s and observed in the villages of Austria, Germany, Italy, and the Tyrol portions of Switzerland, among other localities in Eastern Europe.

Approximately an hour before bedtime, nervous children queued up by the front door, anxiously awaiting the arrival of the saintly bishop and his fearsome companion. Nowadays, gullible children would be overjoyed to learn of Santa's impending visit, anticipating a hearty cuddle from the jolly gentleman, but children back in the day cringed at the sight of the bishop. As soon as Saint Nicholas – usually a family friend in disguise – strode through the front door, the children were inundated with one Biblical question after another, a wintertime oral examination now known as the "Catechism interrogation."

Krampus' persistent taunting only made the experience all the more terrorizing. The growling and hissing creature (a relative or second neighbor) paced to and fro, smacking its birch switch against the palm of its furry hand with a glint in its eye. The creature added to the tension with its vile threats. Krampus warned the children, "Err in your response, and you shall be my prize! For so long, I have yearned for a companion in Hell."

In some cases, Krampus' presence only contributed to the nerves of the interrogated child. They stuttered and stumbled with their words until they could speak no more, which earned them a succession of hard spanks on the behind. Mostly, however, Krampus served more as an incentive, for passing the bishop's test and expelling the demon was regarded by many children as a badge of honor. As a way to soften the trepidation induced by such an activity, the child was awarded a sweet or a piece of fruit for every accurate response.

When children, particularly the older ones, began to grow hardened to the visits of this unlikely duo, parents boosted the theatrics to the next level. Krampus started to loot kitchen cupboards, even smashing an old plate or two for effect. The rowdy beast also began to flirt and act lasciviously towards the female members of the household, as well as engage in mock scuffles with patriarchs and older brothers who had previously been apprised of the situation.

Occasionally, even when the child passed the examination with flying colors, Krampus broke the code and attempted to seize the startled child. This was when the bishop conveniently intervened, wrapping his arm around the child and banishing the demon with a wave of his crosier.

At times, it was not the bishop, but a rare third member of the party, who interceded on the child's behalf. This was either the *Korblträger*, or "basket carrier," a small, elderly gentleman clad in a gray coat, puckered, knee-length pants, and a Tyrolean hat (an ensemble referred to as a "tracht"), or an *Engel* (Angel), a winged young maiden between the ages of 8 and 18. With a dramatic exhale, Krampus swung his flaccid sack over his back and flounced out the door. This twist most likely lends to the modern masses' perception of Krampus, that is – a greasy and conniving Christmas villain that is not to be trusted.

This seemingly archaic tradition continued unto at least the latter half of the 20th century, and it is most likely still practiced in some Alpine villages today. Consider this 1975 account provided by author John J. Honigmann, which illustrates his visit to a local home in Altirdning, Styria, on the eve of Saint Nicholas Day: "Frightened by the visitor's appearance, the two-year-old boy at once began to cry and was immediately taken upstairs by his mother. But no relief was offered to the older children... It was plain that the children, as they knew they were expected to do, tried resolutely to control their fear, despite the almost constant menacing threats of the irrepressible, noisy Krampus."

The following list, arranged by author Molly Carter, breaks down the interactions of the children (in relation to their age) and Nicholas Play performers in detail:

> "...children graduate from one type of interaction to another as they age...each level they advance to involves closer physical proximity...to the Krampus...
>
> 1. Infants: held in parents' arms facing away from the mummers, and removed once they start crying.
>
> 2. Toddlers: facing the [performers], but held in the protective embrace of a parent seated behind the corner table...
>
> 3. Ages four to 12: seated behind the table facing the mummers next to a parent, sometimes called out to stand before [Saint Nicholas] and Krampus while being interrogated.
>
> 4. Teens: standing and moving freely about the room. At this age, boys may play the role of Krampus themselves, and girls may tussle with them in the

playful, flirtatious manner characteristic of parade settings. Boys and girls may also choose not to participate at all."

To this day, some parents firmly believe that this meticulously structured system improves their children's chances of becoming responsible and respectable citizens who regularly contribute to society, a concept the locals call *"Erziehung."* In 1993, Karin Norman, a professor of Social Anthropology at the University of Stockholm, conducted research on the roots and evolution of the Saint Nicholas cult and Krampus traditions in Linden, Bavaria, in which she expands on the effects of integrating these wintertime traditions into the practice of *Erziehung*. Professor Norman wrote, *"Erziehung* is regarded as the process of separating the person from an amorphous nature, the good from the potentially evil, through a technique of teaching and learning that combines intricate forms of praise and punishment. It operates progressively through the institutions of family, kindergarten, school, and church. Notions of order and freedom are closely linked. People believe that through proper upbringing and education, a child will become a socially acceptable being, an orderly and free person... it is only through this process of upbringing that one can become human, [or] *ein richtieger Mensch* (a real or true person)."

Thus, it appears that the Christians were largely responsible for the expansion of the Krampus cult, so the Catholic Church's ongoing mission to omit Krampus from the Christmas pantheon can only be described as confounding. Conservative Catholics, who began to voice their disapproval of the character as early as the 1100s, criticized their fellow Christians for including such an ungodly subject in what were supposed to be sacrosanct traditions. Not only were they disgusted by Krampus' resemblance to the devil, they found the carousing and debauchery that often ensued utterly reprehensible.

Krampus Leaves the Alps

"Krampus, Krampus,

Have you any souls?

Yes, sir, yes, sir, three bags full.

Those who are cheaters,

And those who like flames,

Those who are naughty boys

Who always pass the blame..." - Author Unknown

As the cult of Krampus continued to spread to other parts of the continent like an indomitable contagion, the character began to take on various forms, each attached to their own origin story. Before proceeding, however, it is important to note that the opinions on whether these figures are regional representations of Krampus or separate entities altogether are divided. Either way, the similarities between Krampus and the following characters are indisputable.

Black Pete, otherwise known as "*Zwarte Piet*," was a character formulated in the Low Countries. Piet was possibly inspired by Eckhard and Oel, the ravens that belonged to Odin, the muse behind Santa Claus, or as the Dutch called him, "*Sinterklaas*." These black birds were more than pets, as they doubled as spies. It was from the intel he received from the ravens that he was able to determine the behavior of his subjects on the mortal realm, both outside and behind closed doors.

A depiction of *Sinterklaas* and Black Pete

In the Middle Ages, the image of *Sinterklaas* was updated to include a demonic beast, which he kept leashed at all times. This contemptible creature – perhaps due to the intercession of conservative Catholics – soon faded into the background.

The concept of a companion for Saint Nicholas was nearly forgotten until halfway into the 19th century, when schoolmaster and author Jan Schenkman published the *Sinterklaas* novel, *Saint Nicholas and His Servant,* in 1850. The servant character in Schenkman's novel, many say, is open to interpretation. He was not given a name and only vaguely described as a young man garbed in the old-fashioned uniform of a page from the 1700s. As most pages from this era were of African descent, many applied this logic to their visualization of the bishop's servant. Some speculate that the servant was modeled after Moorish slaves, as depicted in 17th and 18th-century fine art. Others insist that Schenkman had Piter – the Ethiopian slave supposedly purchased and freed by the bishop – in mind. Then, there are those who label the ambiguous servant a scion of Satan. Many have also come to question whether or not the Servant actually hailed from Africa or was dark-skinned by birth. Some suggest that the Servant was "black" not because of skin, but because of his mode of entry through the chimney, which left him smothered in soot. Whatever the case, given the popularity of Schenkman's novel, other local authors took the concept of an African servant and ran with it. The name *"Zwarte Piet"* appeared for the first time in print in a children's book published in 1891.

Up until the Second World War, *Zwarte Piet* was depicted as a stern disciplinarian who punished badly behaved children. Like Krampus, *Piet* flogged naughty children and threatened to carry them off in his sack. These days, however, the role of Black Pete has been diluted to that of a secondary gift-giver. He is much milder in character, and he no longer dispensed whippings or threats. Instead, the young man, still donning the fluffy cap, ruffled collar, and the rest of his 16th century page costume, assists in carrying and presenting the gifts to children.

Another companion is *Knecht Rupert*, also referred to as "Slave" or "Farmhand Rupert," a fabled character produced by German lore. Of all the names on the list, Rupert is said to bear one of the closest (if not almost identical) resemblances to Krampus, excluding its Protestant roots, as opposed to Catholic roots. Rupert made his first appearance as one of Christkindl's earthly "Dark Helpers" in a Christmas-themed German play that debuted in 1668.

Rupert comes in three shapes. In most accounts, Rupert is the spitting image of Krampus as a half-goat, half-human creature equipped with horns and a lolling tongue. In other accounts, he is seen as a crooked-backed, elderly man enveloped in a furry, hooded dark robe adorned with bells, and an unruly, silvery beard that flowed to his ankles. Slung over his shoulder is a bag stuffed with coal, and in his fist, either a short bundle, or a staff made of birch rods. Occasionally, Rupert is also depicted as a small, elfin man dressed in shabby brown rags.

Similar to the catechism interrogations conducted by Saint Nicholas and Krampus, Rupert initially joined Christkindl on his yearly visits to German youths. In later accounts, however, Rupert began to appear on his own on, knocking on front doors on the 6th of December, rather than the 5th of December. Though Rupert continued to make his rounds on the feast day of Saint Nicholas, the Biblical element of the interrogation was gradually removed and substituted with questions regarding the child's behavior throughout the year.

The French had two versions of the Krampus character. The first, *Le Père Fouettard*, or in English, "Father Whipper," was traditionally observed in Nord-Pas-de-Calais, Lorraine, and Wallonia, Belgium. Like the second version of *Knecht Rupert*, Father Whipper is described as an elderly (and sometimes, middle-aged) sage-type with a jet-black beard, dressed in chocolate-brown robes edged with matching black fur.

The customs surrounding this French Krampus pairs the Grinch-like *Père Fouettard* with the bounteous Saint Nicholas. On the 5th of December, the pair traveled to the homes of every French boy and girl, upon which they examined a checklist for good behavior, usually prepared by the guardians in the household. Only those who have done well in their studies, prayed dutifully, and listened to their parents were rewarded with handfuls of chocolates. The disobedient were not whipped with a birch rod bundle, but a martinet – a "scourge-like whip" usually made with horsehair, and at times, a weighty sack filled with ashes.

The intriguing *Père Fouettard* comes with two different origin stories. Some say Father Whipper and the Butcher – an antagonist in one of the miracles most commonly associated with the bishop saint – are one and the same. This tale, which began to circulate around the continent in 1150, tells of a wicked butcher who abducted three hungry children, chopped them into small pieces, and tossed them into a massive pickling barrel to preserve their flesh. The saint, who was informed by the Heavens of this atrocity that same evening, showed up to the butcher shop the next day, where he promptly resurrected the three boys.

Immediately, the butcher, who was himself starving on account of the famine, attempted to explain himself, but the bishop rebuffed him and condemned him to 10 lifetimes in hell. In certain accounts, however, the bishop gave the butcher the opportunity to redeem himself. To demonstrate his remorse and his renewed piety, the butcher was transformed into Father Whipper to serve as Saint Nicholas' minion.

The second origin story involves the 1552 Siege of Metz, a year-long battle in a lengthy war that France's King Henry II waged against the Holy Roman Empire. Locals protesting the oppressive Holy Roman Emperor, Charles V, poured into the streets. Those who partook in the procession paraded around an enormous effigy carved in the likeness of the emperor as spectators hurled decaying crops and moldy bread at the statue, which was eventually set alight in a bonfire. *The History Collection* describes the second half of the Father Whipper character: "At the same time, the tanners of Metz had created a grotesque character who punishes children.

The two separate effigies somehow married themselves together in the popular mind, and became incorporated into the role of *Le Pere Fouettard.*"

Hans Trapp is another Christmas villain whom many consider France's second alternative to Krampus. The character, born in the Alsace and Lorraine regions of France, also played the part of Saint Nicholas' companion, and while he, too, punished disrespectful children, his origin story is entirely unique.

Most notably, Sir Trapp was in part modeled after Hans von Troth, a 6'6" German knight of ill repute. Similar to von Troth, Sir Trapp was a notoriously rich and powerful 15th century knight and landowner who resided in the heartland of Alsace, and unlike Saint Nicholas, who was born in an affluent family and famed for his philanthropy, Trapp was ill-tempered, selfish, pitiless, and endlessly vain. He was never satisfied with his mountain of wealth, so he regularly swindled those around him to not only maintain, but enlarge his treasury. Trapp was supposedly so desperate to hold onto his wealth that he kowtowed to the Devil and engaged in occult worship.

Trapp's innumerable transgressions were eventually discovered by the Pope, who then ordered the seizure of all of the knight's riches, lands, and possessions, and excommunicated him from the Church on charges of sacrilege. The disgraced knight attempted to live amongst the citizens of Alsace, but the locals – particularly the poor – remembered the torment they endured and shunned him. Despised, unwanted, and all alone, Trapp left France and lived as a nomad for years until he finally found refuge on Mount Geisberg in Bavaria. The makeshift hut he constructed for himself was made primarily out of birch, believed to be a callback to Krampus.

As the years progressed, Trapp spiraled further and further into his lunacy, supposedly fueled by his increased veneration of Satan, until he began to crave human flesh. In time, he plumped himself up with straw, so as to emulate a scarecrow, and began to rove around the Bavarian countryside.

One day, Trapp spotted the small, but clear-cut figure of a young shepherd boy in the distance, no older than the age of 10. The aspiring cannibal quickly positioned himself against a fixture of sticks. As soon as the young shepherd walked past him, Trapp lunged forth and skewered him with a birch stick that he had whittled into a spear. Then, like the Butcher of Myra, Trapp cut up the corpse into several pieces and cooked the hunks of meat over a campfire.

Before Trapp could dig in, a blinding bolt of lightning shot out of the sky and smote him, killing him instantly. It was God, they say, who sent the fatal bolt, and He who placed the curse upon the dishonorable knight. From there on out, Trapp's spirit – still clothed in his scarecrow costume – was made to accompany Saint Nicholas on his yearly visits to the home of French and Bavarian children. Mischievous children were warned never to lower their guards during the first two weeks of December, for Trapp was still on the prowl, itching to take his first bite of human flesh.

Otto von Reinsberg-Düringsfeld's depiction of Trapp visiting children in Alsace

Then there's the Icelandic Krampus, which literally rears its head during Christmastime, celebrated between the 23rd of December and the 6th of January. Most Icelandic children know of Grýla, the revolting ogress often described as a hybrid of a troll and a goat. Grýla lived in the bleakest part of the snow-covered mountains with her third husband, 13 boys (now known as the "Yule Lads"), and a large, beefy black cat. Every year, on the 23rd of December, Grýla, the Yule Lads, and their pet cat flock to civilization, the mother in pursuit of insubordinate children for supper and the lads on a mission to wreak mayhem. Fortunately, disobedient children who found themselves in Grýla's grasp could repent, and if they were sincere, Grýla had no choice but to release them.

David Stanley's picture of a depiction of Grýla and her husband

Some historians believe that Grýla is an offshoot of Krampus, perhaps even a daughter. Others claim that Krampus can be found in each and every one of the 13 lads – Sheep-Cote Clod, Gully Gawk, Stubby, Spoon Licker, Pot Scraper, Bowl Licker, Door Slammer, Skyr Gobbler, Sausage Swiper, Window Peeper, Door Sniffer, Meat Hook, and Candle Beggar. Then, there are those who link Krampus to the so-called "Christmas Cat." Those who failed to present their family and friends with a new article of clothing, whether adult or child, were devoured by this man-eating feline.

Krampus' reach across Europe certainly stretched far and wide. In other parts of Germany, Krampus is also referred to as *Bullerklaus*, and in Bavaria, Krampus is referred to as *Klaubauf.* Slovenia and Switzerland have their own takes on Krampus too, known to the locals as *Parkejl*, and *Schmutzli*, respectively. In certain remote Austrian villages, the daunting Christmas Devil is also accompanied by an equally dubious character dubbed the "Antlered Wild Man."

Europe's Krampus craze began to fizzle out towards the second half of the 17th century, but the wintertime beast was once again thrust into the spotlight in the 19th century. In 1810, brothers Wilhelm and Jacob Grimm released the first in what would be a carefully curated, spectacular collection of ancient German folktales. Krampus as people now recognize it was mentioned by name in one of Jacob's chronicles, entitled *Deutsche Mythologie,* or *Teutonic Mythology*, published in 1835.

Meanwhile, the legend of Krampus, which had been brought to the New World by Germanic and Dutch immigrants based in Pennsylvania, Maryland, and Indiana, began to gain momentum in North America for the first time. There, the Krampus character was not marketed by its name, but rather as "Pelznickel," also referred to as Belsnickel, Kriskrinkle, Beltznickle, and Pelsnichol. Pelznickel and his tale was broken out of the folklore predominantly circulated along the Rhine in southwestern Germany, as well as the Saarland and the Odenwald region of Baden-Wurttemberg.

Pelznickel's name was a combination of two German words: *bels (pelz)*, or in English, "fur," and *nickel,* a nod to Saint Nicholas. Similar to *Knecht Rupert,* Pelznickel was a fusion of Saint Nicholas the rewarder, and Krampus the punisher – by then an age-old dynamic – but unlike the farmhand, Pelznickel was not portrayed as a beast, but man. He, too, stalked the streets of the German and Dutch-American communities for bad children, dressed in a soiled fur cloak, and either deer antlers, or a crown garnished with branches and dead foliage on his head, and all visible limbs smeared with charcoal. The unkempt, bearded figure was also sometimes seen with a creepy wooden mask carved and painted by hand. In some accounts, Pelznickel also disguised himself in a scraggly wig and women's clothing, hence his lesser-known nicknames, the "Christmas Woman" and the "Christmas Witch."

In line with the generic version of Krampus, naughty children were swatted with birch switches. Swattings from Pelznickel, however, were the least of their worries. Borrowing from the legend of Krampus, errant children were also at risk of being dragged off into the woods, never to be seen again. Still, there remained one ray of hope; children could vindicate themselves by following a series of humiliating orders, which included jumping, singing, dancing, reciting poems, and other tricks, not unlike those given by the Lord of Misrule, or the King of Fools. Those who behaved throughout the year were duly rewarded with candies, sponge cakes, and nuts, as well as socks, mittens, and small handcrafted trinkets.

In *Christmas in Pennsylvania: A Folk Cultural Study,* authors Alfred Shoemaker and Don Yoder described a typical visit from the Pelznickel: "The annual visitor would make his appearance some hours after dark, thoroughly disguised, especially the face, which would sometimes be covered with a hideously ugly phiz... He or she would be equipped with an ample sack about the shoulders filled with cakes, nuts, and fruits, and a long hazel switch which was supposed to have some kind of charm in it as well as a sting…One would scatter the goodies upon the floor, and then the scramble would begin by the delighted children, and the other hand would ply the switch upon the backs of the excited youngsters – who would not show a wince, but had it been parental discipline there would have been screams to reach a long distance."

Today, Pelznickel is still celebrated, and the traditions are still practiced in many Pennsylvania Dutch communities, but despite Pelznickel's impact in the Dutch-American communities, the popularity of these figures was seriously limited by numerous factors. Christopher Bickel, a contributor of *Dangerous Minds,* explained, "It [has] been theorized that the Krampus lore was brought over to the US by German-speaking immigrants, but never took hold on American shores due to [the] anti-German sentiment over the First and Second World Wars...but that Santa Claus did catch on, because he made a great mascot for [various industries including] the Coca-Cola Company. A devil who beats children isn't really going to be an effective soda pop pitchman. A jolly fat guy who hands out gifts? Perfect."

Krampus in the Modern Age

"...You're going to your doom,

You're going straight to Hell,

Krampus knows you're a ne'er-do-well...

You'll get beaten with a stick,

Not get gifts from Old Saint Nick.

Fright, fright, fright,

Krampus comes tonight!" – "Doom, Doom, Doom," Author Unknown

The cult of Krampus may have been stunted in the United States, but back where it originally started, the movement surrounding the Christmas Devil continued to spread deeper into Eastern Europe. In the years leading up to the mid-19th century, a tradition began wherein families, friends, and neighbors traded *Krampuskarten* amongst themselves. In short, *Krampuskarten,* normally accompanied by the phrase, "Gruß vom Krampus" ("Greetings from the Krampus"), became a more disturbing and mature form of the conventional Christmas card.

An early 20th century postcard depicting Krampus and a child

In 1890, the Austrian government surrendered dominion over the country's postcard manufacturing industries, which led this niche and soon-to-be prosperous sector to its sudden boom. Greeting card producers across the country pounced on the opportunity to commercialize Krampus, which seemed to growing in popularity, and churned out *Krampuskarten* in droves. The most common imagery portrayed in these exquisitely illustrated postcards, which remain high-priced collectibles to this day, featured Krampus closing in on children, as well as the beast punishing the children in a variety of ways, inspired by actual stories passed down the grapevine.

In the early 20th century, artists began to show the once family-friendly beast in a lewder light. Krampus started to badger and bedevil full-fledged adults with practical jokes and mischief during *Krampuslauf*, a practice now referred to as "*Kramperltratzn*" or "*Tuifltratzen*," the suffix of the term, another word for "*reizen*," meaning "to tease or to aggravate," as well as "to allure and to excite erotically." Such postcards featured Krampus either propositioning or drooling after housewives and young maidens.

Towards the latter half of the 1900s, particularly during the age of the hippies, enterprising artists introduced Krampus to the BDSM scene. In one such greeting card, Krampus can be seen spanking bound and skimpily dressed women bent over his lap, and vice versa. Another sexually charged postcard features the obscene imagery of a shackled young woman, turned away from the audience, kneeling before Krampus as the beast suggestively grabs a fistful of her hair.

Other adult-themed *Krampuskarten* featured generic illustrations of a Krampus up to no good, paired with chilling, but catchy rhymes. The following are a few examples collected by Jessie Strasbaugh, a contributor for the *Oxford Dictionary Blog:*

"Mit Bomben und Granaten soll dich der Teufel braten!" ("The devil will fry you with bombs and grenades!").

"Seid ihr heuer brav gewesen? Sonst krieg ihr's mit dem Krampusbesen!" ("Have you been good today? If not, you will get hit with the Krampus' switch!").

"Geh mach dei' Fensterl auf, der Krampus wart' scho' drauf!" ("Go open the window; the Krampus is waiting for you!").

Given the unveiling of Krampus' sexual side, it is not difficult to imagine why the controversial creature, along with *Krampuslauf* and *Krampusnacht,* was outlawed by conservative political parties in Austria shortly after the 1923 elections. Krampus' main opponents – as maintained by a 1934 article, "Krampus Disliked in Fascist Austria," published by *The New York Times* – were the fascist Christian Social Party and the Dolfuss-run Vaterlandische Front, or "Fatherland's Front." The anti-Communist political parties, it is said, disapproved of Krampus' devilish qualities, which they likened to the "Red Devil Soviet Union." More importantly, the political parties despised the creature since it was, as the article put it, "the work of the wicked Social Democrats."

The Austrian Catholic Union parroted the conservatives' sentiments, arguing that the Christmas season – which had become too deeply invested in a pagan and irrelevant character – was losing its meaning. They also cited the borderline pornographic *Krampuskarten* that was then experiencing a surge in popularity and branded the beast a threat to the innocence of Christian children and adults alike. On top of the ban, the Catholic Union urged Christians across Austria and beyond to initiate a complete and thorough boycott of all Krampus merchandise, from *Krampuskarten* and Krampus-related literature to even chocolates and biscuits that bore even the slightest resemblance to the wintertime fiend. The crackdown on Krampus dances and parties was so severe that even those who wished to dress up as Santa Claus were first made to acquire an official license granted to them by the mayor. The article noted, "The police have been given orders to see that Santa Claus, duly licensed, behaves himself properly, and to arrest the devil [Krampus] at sight."

The smear campaign against Krampus continued well into the 1950s. On December 13, 1953, *The Sunday Mail* of Brisbane released an article entitled "Christmas in Austria," which told readers, "Last week, the head of Vienna's kindergarten system warned parents that the effect of an interview with Krampus might well leave their children scarred for life. In a leaflet called 'Krampus is an Evil Man,' Dr. Ernst Kotbauer urged that his children be freed of the frightful cross examiner. A Vienna daily rushed to Dr. Kotbauer's support: 'There is too much fear in this world already – unemployment, high taxes, not to mention the atom bomb. Let us begin by throwing out the Krampus."

Notwithstanding the attempts to suppress Krampus, the notorious Christmas Devil persevered and is now in the midst of yet another major resurgence, mainly in the United States. Author, illustrator, and graphic designer Monte Beauchamp is now credited with rekindling the flames. Beauchamp, as the story goes, became fascinated by the Austrian beast at some point between the late 1990s and the early 2000s, when he was shown an enchanting collection of vintage *Krampuskarten* dating back to the 19th and early 20th centuries by an unnamed modern-day treasure hunter. Beauchamp then purchased these postcards and published them in two issues of *Blab!,* an anthology of various comics and graphic design that he edited, and reprinted them again in two books, one released in 2004 and the other in 2010.

Much to Beauchamp's astonishment, these works received an overwhelmingly positive response, which soon attracted the attention of a gallery director from Santa Monica, California. Together, Beauchamp and the director teamed up to organize an exhibit dedicated to various artistic renditions of these famous *Krampuskarten*. This exhibit, now a semiannual event, continues to thrive to this day. Beauchamp also continues to receive licensing requests for his Krampus postcards.

Moreover, in Austria and other parts of Eastern Europe, *Krampusnacht* has been modernized, and it is now celebrated with even more gusto. In Schladming, Styria, for instance, more than 1,200 Austrian Krampus folk performers gather each year for the annual *Krampuslauf.*

Lukas Niederberger's picture of people dressed as St. Nicholas and Krampus

Perhaps not surprisingly, cases of Krampus-related festivities spiraling out of control are not unusual. In 2015, for instance, five teenagers were hospitalized for moderate to severe bruises and injuries inflicted upon them by overexcited Krampus performers. Journalist Michael Karas of North Jersey's *The Record* recounted his own experience at a traditional *Krampuslauf* in 2014, writing, "The narrow streets in the Old City section of Salzburg were packed with pedestrians as the Krampusse stomped through. Many people were caught unaware and reacted with terror. Some would flee and try to seek refuge in a shop or restaurant, only to be pursued by a determined Krampus...At times we were chased, jostled, and struck, but compared with the brutality we witnessed, it was obvious we had been spared the full brunt of what [the Krampusse] could muster."

This, as Karas explains, was soon about to change: "[A new wave of Krampusse] began to growl as they approached and held their switches at the ready. We backed away slowly, but the Krampusse were soon upon us delivering a swift beating to our shins and thighs that left us reeling...Back in the safety of our guesthouse, under multiple layers of thermal pants and wool socks, we discovered a number of raised welts and small bruises on our legs...As we marveled at our ruptured blood vessels, it became painfully obvious that while we think of ourselves as 'good' people, there was now overwhelming evidence to the contrary..."

Online Resources

Other books about Christmas by Charles River Editors

Other books about Christianity by Charles River Editors

Other books about Krampus on Amazon

Further Reading

Leafloor, L. (2015, December 3). Santa's Horned Helper: The Fearsome Legend of Krampus, Christmas Punisher. Retrieved December 18, 2018, from https://www.ancient-origins.net/myths-legends/santa-s-horned-helper-fearsome-legend-krampus-christmas-punisher-004799

Zimmerman, J. (2017, December 7). 9 Facts About Krampus, St. Nick's Demonic Companion. Retrieved December 18, 2018, from http://mentalfloss.com/article/71999/9-facts-about-krampus-st-nicks-demonic-companion

Editors, L. 2. (2017, November 8). 25 Creepy Cool Facts About Krampus. Retrieved December 18, 2018, from https://list25.com/25-creepy-cool-facts-about-krampus/

O'Connor, K. (2015, December 3). 12 facts about Krampus. Retrieved December 18, 2018, from https://www.chron.com/entertainment/slideshow/11-facts-about-Krampus-121510.php

Van Duser, N. (2018, December 5). 10 SURPRISING FACTS ABOUT KRAMPUS THE CHRISTMAS DEMON. Retrieved December 18, 2018, from https://www.altpress.com/features/krampus-facts-myths-krampusnacht/2/

Basu, T. (2018, December 5). Who is Krampus? Explaining the horrific Christmas beast. Retrieved December 18, 2018, from https://news.nationalgeographic.com/news/2013/12/131217-krampus-christmas-santa-devil/

Baines, W. (2017). 6 Terrifying Facts About Santa's Horned Helper. Retrieved December 18, 2018, from https://www.beliefnet.com/love-family/holidays/6-terrifying-facts-about-santas-horned-helper.aspx?p=3

Editors, A. T. (2018, November 2). Meet Krampus — The Terrifying Anti-Santa Who Eats Bad Children. Retrieved December 18, 2018, from https://allthatsinteresting.com/krampus

McCarthy, T. (2015, December 4). Who Is Krampus? 5 Things To Know About The 'Christmas Devil' Ahead Of The 2015 Horror Movie. Retrieved December 18, 2018, from https://www.ibtimes.com/who-krampus-5-things-know-about-christmas-devil-ahead-2015-horror-movie-2211614

Editors, K. (2017). WHO IN HELL IS KRAMPUS? Retrieved December 18, 2018, from http://www.krampus.com/who-is-krampus.php

Editors, R. (2018, December 17). Krampus. Retrieved December 18, 2018, from https://www.revolvy.com/page/Krampus

Editors, V. S. (2017). PERCHTENLÄUFE: SALZBURG'S PAGAN HERITAGE. Retrieved December 18, 2018, from http://www.visit-salzburg.net/travel/perchten.htm

Editors, T. C. (2017). FEAR THE AUSTRIAN PERCHTEN: PAGAN TRADITIONS IN THE ALPS, PART I. Retrieved December 18, 2018, from http://www.tourmycountry.com/austria/perchtenpagancustom1.htm

Ward, C. (2010, December 23). 10 Fun Facts About Krampus, the Christmas Demon. Retrieved December 18, 2018, from https://www.toplessrobot.com/2010/12/10_fun_facts_about_krampus_the_christmas_demon.php

Dimick, C. (2010, December 22). Krampus' Claws Are Coming To Kill. Retrieved December 18, 2018, from http://rdhorrorproject.blogspot.com/2010/12/krampus-claws-are-coming-to-kill.html

Hirsch, D. (2009, December 5). 25 Days of Weird Christmas: Better watch out, Krampus is coming to town. Retrieved December 18, 2018, from https://blog.sfgate.com/culture/2009/12/05/25-days-of-weird-christmas-better-watch-out-krampus-is-coming-to-town/

Billock, J. (2015, December 4). The Origin of Krampus, Europe's Evil Twist on Santa. Retrieved December 18, 2018, from https://www.smithsonianmag.com/travel/krampus-could-come-you-holiday-season-180957438/

Editors, A. K. (2013, December 6). Krampus: The Holiday Devil. Retrieved December 18, 2018, from http://associationofparanormalstudy.com/2013/12/06/krampus-the-holiday-devil/

Little, B. (2017, November 23). HOW KRAMPUS, THE CHRISTMAS 'DEVIL,' BECAME COOL. Retrieved December 18, 2018, from https://www.nationalgeographic.com.au/people/how-krampus-the-christmas-devil-became-cool.aspx

Faletto, J. (2015, December 3). Meet Krampus, The Terrifying Anti-Santa. Retrieved December 18, 2018, from https://curiosity.com/topics/meet-krampus-the-anti-santa-curiosity/

Taylor, A. (2013, December 3). Krampus: Saint Nicholas' Dark Companion. Retrieved December 18, 2018, from https://www.theatlantic.com/photo/2013/12/krampus-saint-nicholas-dark-companion/100639/

Ridenour, A. (2013, November 29). The Truth About Krampus. Retrieved December 19, 2018, from https://www.atlasobscura.com/articles/the-truth-about-krampus

Editors, M. (2016). Krampus. Retrieved December 19, 2018, from https://mythology.net/demons/krampus/

Sullivan, K. (2017, February 27). Krampus, Son of Hel: The Ancient Origins of the Christmas Devil. Retrieved December 19, 2018, from https://www.ancient-origins.net/history-ancient-traditions/krampus-son-hel-ancient-origins-christmas-devil-007627

Little, B. (2018, December 5). Meet Krampus, the Christmas Devil Who Punishes Naughty Children. Retrieved December 19, 2018, from https://www.history.com/news/krampus-christmas-legend-origin

Carlton, G. (2015). Unpacking Krampus: Santa's Evil Partner In Crime. Retrieved December 19, 2018, from https://www.ranker.com/list/history-of-christmas-krampus/genevieve-carlton

Kelly, D. (2016). The untold truth of Krampus. Retrieved December 19, 2018, from https://www.grunge.com/99592/untold-truth-krampus/

Martin, E. (2016, December 5). THE HISTORY OF KRAMPUS. Retrieved December 19, 2018, from https://www.trazeetravel.com/the-history-of-krampus/

Muckerman, A. (2018, December 18). Is Christmas demon Krampus losing his edge? Retrieved December 19, 2018, from https://www.pri.org/stories/2018-12-18/christmas-demon-krampus-losing-his-edge

Lamb, R. (2015, December 4). Where did Krampus come from? Retrieved December 19, 2018, from https://people.howstuffworks.com/culture-traditions/cultural-traditions/where-did-krampus-come-from.htm

Editors, G. W. (2015, December 2). Krampus, the Christmas Devil of Alpine Europe. Retrieved December 19, 2018, from https://www.german-way.com/krampus-the-christmas-devil-of-alpine-europe/

Nadel, D. (2017, December 22). A Brief History of Krampus in America. Retrieved December 19, 2018, from https://owlcation.com/social-sciences/A-Brief-History-of-Krampus-in-America

Editors, S. L. (2017). Https://www.salzburgerland.com/en/krampus-and-perchten/. Retrieved December 19, 2018, from https://www.salzburgerland.com/en/krampus-and-perchten/

Auryn, M. (2018, December 4). A Brief History of The Krampus. Retrieved December 19, 2018, from https://www.patheos.com/blogs/matauryn/2018/12/04/krampus/

Hoeller, S. C. (2017, December 5). The story behind 'Krampus,' Santa's demonic helper who exists to scare children into being good. Retrieved December 19, 2018, from https://www.thisisinsider.com/what-is-krampus-saint-nicholaus-2016-12#krampus-is-so-insanely-scary-that-he-was-actually-banned-a-few-times-alternatively-by-the-catholic-church-and-the-austrian-government-and-later-during-wwii-for-allegedly-being-a-product-of-social-democrats-12

Editors, R. B. (2012, December 19). The History of the Krampus Card. Retrieved December 19, 2018, from https://blog.redbubble.com/2012/12/the-history-of-the-krampus-card/

Editors, T. D. (2018, November 12). What is the Krampuslauf? Retrieved December 19, 2018, from https://www.traveldudes.org/travel-videos/what-krampuslauf/141600

Sokol, T. (2018, December 5). The Anti-Christmas Spirit of Krampus. Retrieved December 19, 2018, from https://www.denofgeek.com/us/culture/krampus/242079/the-anti-christmas-spirit-of-krampus

Ferranti, S. (2016, December 27). The strange and sinister story of the Christmas Krampus. Retrieved December 19, 2018, from https://www.dazeddigital.com/artsandculture/article/34144/1/the-strange-and-sinister-story-of-the-christmas-krampus

Harrington, J. (2017). THE HISTORY OF KRAMPUS'S GAL-PAL, FRAU PERCHTA: THE BELLY-SLITTER. Retrieved December 20, 2018, from https://totallythebomb.com/the-history-of-krampuss-gal-pal-frau-perchta-the-belly-slitter

Blitz, M. (2014, December 11). KRAMPUS, THE CHRISTMAS DEMON. Retrieved December 20, 2018, from http://www.todayifoundout.com/index.php/2014/12/krampus-christmas-demon/

Hurd, R. (2012, December 24). Horror for the Holidays: Santa, Krampus, and the Dark Divine. Retrieved December 20, 2018, from http://www.teemingbrain.com/2012/12/24/horror-for-the-holidays-santa-krampus-and-the-dark-divine/

Hart, A. (2016, December 25). KRAMPUSNACHT. Retrieved December 20, 2018, from https://www.rattle.com/krampusnacht-by-ann-hart/

Carter, M. (2016, February). PERCHTEN AND KRAMPUSSE: LIVING MASK TRADITIONS IN AUSTRIA AND BAVARIA. Retrieved December 20, 2018, from http://etheses.whiterose.ac.uk/14431/1/Carter.Perchten-Krampusse.Thesis.Feb.2016-ethesis.pdf

Editors, N. M. (2017). HEL (GODDESS). Retrieved December 20, 2018, from https://norse-mythology.org/gods-and-creatures/giants/hel/

Editors, A. P. (2018, March 26). Hel – Loki's Terrible Daughter And Goddess Of The Land Of Dead. Retrieved December 20, 2018, from http://www.ancientpages.com/2018/03/26/hel-lokis-terrible-daughter-and-goddess-of-the-land-of-dead/

Editors, S. L. (2015, December 28). Krampus, Hel and Niflheim. Retrieved December 20, 2018, from https://mysecretlore.wordpress.com/2015/12/28/krampus-hel-and-niflheim/

Bustamonte, S. (2018, December 4). Krampus Spaß. Retrieved December 20, 2018, from https://wildhunt.org/2018/12/the-murky-origin-of-the-krampus.html

Editors, K. N. (2014, March 28). Krampus: Santa's Evil Counterpart. Retrieved December 20, 2018, from https://knowledgenuts.com/2014/03/28/krampus-santas-evil-counterpart/

Harrington, L. A. (2017, December 8). KRAMPUS, The Christmas Devil. Retrieved December 20, 2018, from http://www.lisanneharrington.com/krampus-the-christmas-devil/

Warner, C. (2016, December 1). Is Krampus Real? The Legend Is Fascinating, Even If The "Christmas Devil" Isn't Based On Truth. Retrieved December 20, 2018, from https://www.bustle.com/articles/197713-is-krampus-real-the-legend-is-fascinating-even-if-the-christmas-devil-isnt-based-on-truth

Editors, R. (2018, December 12). Perchta. Retrieved December 20, 2018, from https://www.revolvy.com/page/Perchta

Editors, T. C. (2017). FEAR THE AUSTRIAN PERCHTEN: PAGAN TRADITIONS IN THE ALPS, PART II. Retrieved December 20, 2018, from http://www.tourmycountry.com/austria/perchtenpagancustom2.htm

Editors, O. G. (2012, December 19). Household Spirits. Retrieved December 20, 2018, from http://owlsgathering.blogspot.com/2012/12/ahousehold-deity-protects-ones-home.html

Editors, W. P. (2018, July 30). Hob & Broom: Household Lore & Traditions. Retrieved December 20, 2018, from http://witchesandpagans.com/pagan-studies-blogs/hob-broom/monsters-in-the-closet-echoes-of-household-spirits.html

Editors, W. P. (2017, August 8). Kobolds: Household Tricksters. Retrieved December 20, 2018, from http://witchesandpagans.com/pagan-studies-blogs/hob-broom/kobolds-household-tricksters.html

Editors, T. (2012). SATYROI. Retrieved December 20, 2018, from https://www.theoi.com/Georgikos/Satyroi.html

Editors, M. (2018, October 1). Faun. Retrieved December 20, 2018, from https://mythology.net/roman/roman-creatures/faun/

Wright, M. S. (2017, August 10). Who Are the Wiccan Horned God and Triple Goddess? Retrieved December 21, 2018, from https://exemplore.com/wicca-witchcraft/Wicca-for-Beginners-Who-Is-the-Horned-God-and-the-Triple-Goddess

Editors, P. P. (2002, May 7). The Great Horned God. Retrieved December 21, 2018, from https://www.paganspath.com/magik/hornedgod.htm

Editors, O. S. (2013, December 5). Krampus, The Christmas Demon. Retrieved December 21, 2018, from http://theotherside.timsbrannan.com/2013/12/krampus-christmas-demon.html

Cichanowicz, L. (2016, November 19). Everything You Need To Know About Krampus, Germany's Scary Christmas Tradition. Retrieved December 21, 2018, from https://theculturetrip.com/europe/germany/articles/everything-you-need-to-know-about-krampus-germanys-scary-christmas-tradition/

Eidt, J. (2016, December 17). Krampus, Wild Nature Spirit, the Christmas Daemon. Retrieved December 21, 2018, from https://www.wilderutopia.com/traditions/krampus-wild-nature-spirit-the-christmas-daemon/

Editors, P. R. (2014, November 30). Light the Yule Log & Crack the Chains: Krampusnacht Traditions. Retrieved December 21, 2018, from https://powderroom.kinja.com/light-the-yule-log-crack-the-chains-krampusnacht-tra-1664905052

Galitzin, M. (2017, January 7). What about Krampus Night? Retrieved December 21, 2018, from https://www.traditioninaction.org/Cultural/C039_Krampus.htm

Editors, E. B. (2017, July 20). Saturnalia. Retrieved December 21, 2018, from https://www.britannica.com/topic/Saturnalia-Roman-festival

Laskow, S. (2017, December 29). The New Year's Feast That Transformed Fools Into Popes and Kings. Retrieved December 21, 2018, from https://www.atlasobscura.com/articles/feast-of-fools-medieval-tradition

Editors, B. P. (2014). Zwarte Piet is Zwarte (black) Klaas. Retrieved December 21, 2018, from https://blackpetehistory.weebly.com/

Tavares, I. (2004, June 28). Black Pete: Analyzing a Racialized Dutch Tradition Through the History of Western Creations of Stereotypes of Black Peoples. Retrieved December 21, 2018, from https://www.humanityinaction.org/knowledgebase/255-black-pete-analyzing-a-racialized-dutch-tradition-through-the-history-of-western-creations-of-stereotypes-of-black-peoples

Editors, P. A. (2014, December 6). THE STORY OF KNECHT RUPRECHT. Retrieved December 21, 2018, from https://www.pretty-attitude.com/blogs/news/55347845-the-story-of-knecht-ruprecht

Editors, O. S. (2016). Knecht Ruprecht (Servant Rupert): 17th Century Germany. Retrieved December 21, 2018, from http://www.oldeworldsantas.com/k-ruprecht.htm

Sahsnotasvriunt, T. A. (2015, October 10). Quick Facts: Knecht Ruprecht, Krampus, Bullerklaas. Retrieved December 21, 2018, from https://paganmeltingpot.wordpress.com/2015/10/10/knecht-ruprecht-krampus-bullerklaas/

Hoare, J. (2016, December 19). Le Père Fouettard: The French Christmas cannibal who serves Santa Claus. Retrieved December 21, 2018, from https://www.historyanswers.co.uk/people-politics/le-pere-fouettard-the-french-christmas-cannibal-who-serves-santa-claus/

Editors, S. K. (2013, January 8). Hans Trapp. Retrieved December 21, 2018, from http://www.scaryforkids.com/hans-trapp/

Nuwer, R. (2013, December 17). Meet the Thirteen Yule Lads, Iceland's Own Mischievous Santa Clauses. Retrieved December 21, 2018, from https://www.smithsonianmag.com/smart-news/meet-the-thirteen-yule-lads-icelands-own-mischievous-santa-clauses-180948162/

Schneck, M. (2018, December 12). What is the Belsnickel? Why is it part of a Pennsylvania Dutch Christmas? Retrieved December 21, 2018, from https://www.pennlive.com/life/2018/12/what_is_the_belsnickel_why_is.html?fbclid=IwAR3vXHZdsXCCXuH5Dd0cRiXliVNqnweJPcNVcTUEfwoFq-FdBWTXqK50wtM

Editors, I. B. (2017). Belsnickel. Retrieved December 21, 2018, from http://www.indobase.com/holidays/christmas/characters/belsnickel.html

Strasbaugh, J. (2012, December 4). Who is the Krampus? Retrieved December 21, 2018, from https://blog.oxforddictionaries.com/2012/12/04/the-krampus/

Editors, W. T. (2015). The Christmas Outlaw. Retrieved December 21, 2018, from https://wordpress.susqu.edu/engl100-17/krampus/early-krampus/

Editors, S. M. (1953, December 13). Christmas in Austria. Retrieved December 21, 2018, from https://trove.nla.gov.au/newspaper/article/100183731?searchTerm=krampus&searchLimits=

Editors, H. B. (2016, December 5). THIS ISN'T YOUR GRANDMA'S KRAMPUSNACHT. Retrieved December 21, 2018, from https://hafuboti.com/2016/12/05/this-isnt-your-grandmas-krampusnacht/

Free Books by Charles River Editors

We have brand new titles available for free most days of the week. To see which of our titles are currently free, click on this link.

Discounted Books by Charles River Editors

We have titles at a discount price of just 99 cents everyday. To see which of our titles are currently 99 cents, click on this link.

Printed in Great Britain
by Amazon